Astronomy For Beginners

A Young Stargazers Guide To The Universe

Children Explore Outer Space Books

SPEEDY PUBLISHING

Speedy Publishing LLC
40 E. Main St. #1156
Newark, DE 19711
www.speedypublishing.com

ASTRONOMY
Fun Facts
(Beginners' Level)

The Universe is probably about 15 billion years old, but the estimations vary.

Light from the sun takes 8 minutes to reach you, thus you see the sun as it was 8 minutes ago. It might have blown up 4 minutes ago and you wouldn't know about it!

Jupiter is heavier than all the other planets put together.

The tallest mountain in the solar system is Olympus Mons, on Mars at a height of about 15 miles, three times the height of Mount Everest. It covers an area about half the size of Spain.

If the sun were the size of a dot on an ordinary-sized letter 'i', then the nearest star would be 10 miles away.

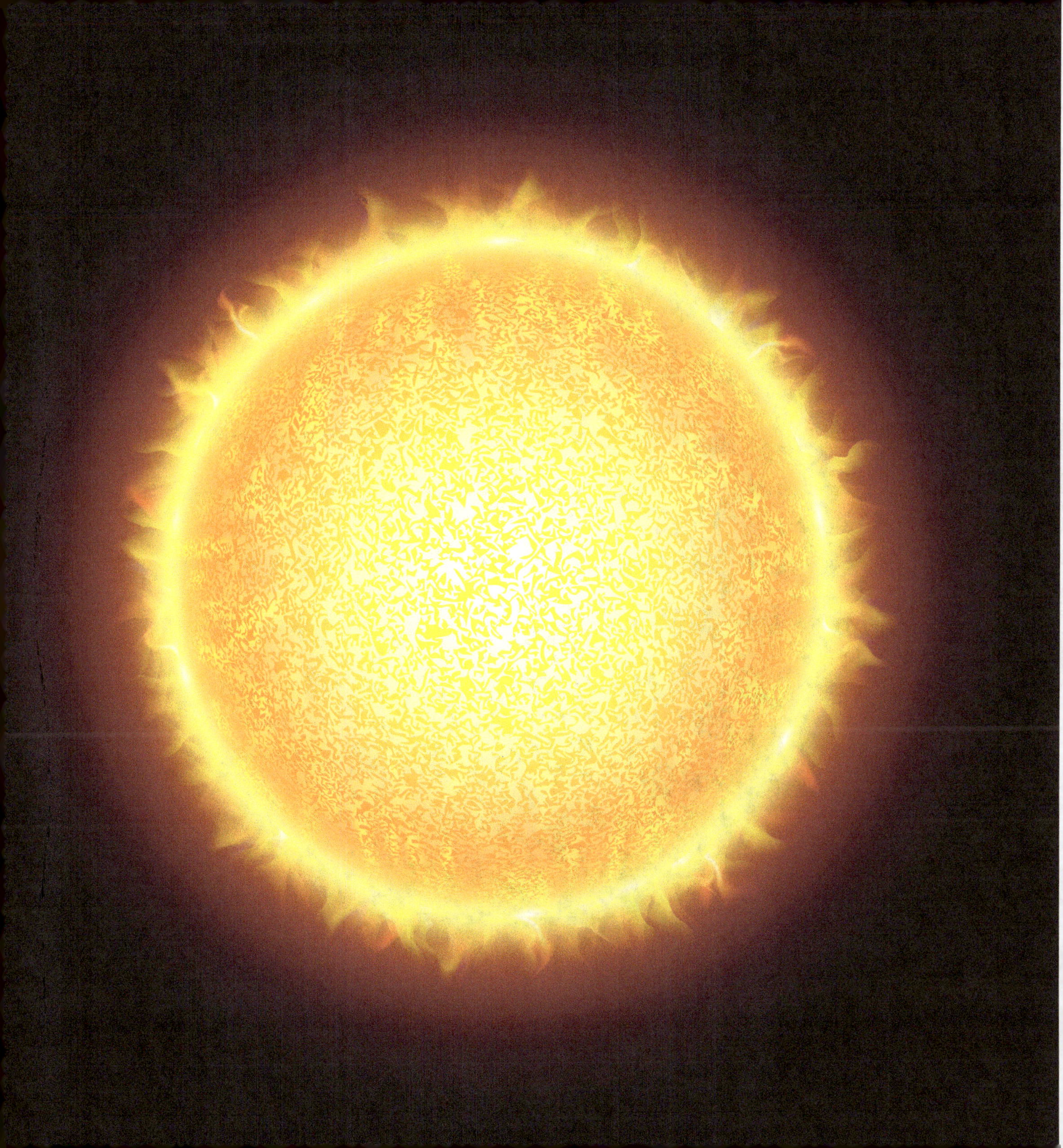

Temperatures on Venus are hot enough to melt lead.

If you stand on the equator, you are spinning at about 1,000 mph in as the Earth turns, as well as charging along at 67,000 mph round the sun.

Great Bear L.
Great Slave L.
CANADA
Greenland
NORTH AMERICA
Ottawa
New York
Washington
UNITED STATES
Mississippi
San Francisco
Los Angeles
MEXICO
G. of Mexico
CUBA
Caracas
VENEZUELA
Cd. de Mexico
Bogota
COLOMBIA
ECUADOR
GUYANA
SURINAME
GUIANA
SOUTH AMERICA
BRAZIL
PERU
BOLIVIA
Lima
ARGENTINA
Santiago
Buenos Aires
URUGUAY
ATLANTIC
OCEAN
IRELAND
London
ICELAND
Solstice
Winter
Dec.

On the equator you are about 3% lighter than at the poles, due to the centrifugal* force of the Earth spinning.

Only one side of the moon ever faces Earth. The moons period of rotation is exactly the same as it's period of orbit.

Saturn is not the only planet with rings- Neptune has it's own ring system.

The Sun, Moon, stars and planets all appear to slowly rise in the East and set in the West each day because the Earth rotates once around its axis every 24 hours.

The Earth orbits the Sun once per year. As it does, the constant tilt of 23.5 degrees of the Earth's rotation axis causes the seasons in the Northern and Southern high latitudes.

The Sun and stars are the same kind of object: huge spheres of hot Hydrogen gas, radiating heat and light. The reason the Sun appears so bright is that it is much, much closer to the Earth than the other stars.

The Moon and planets in our Solar System are cool spheres like the Earth, physically much smaller than stars. They shine because of reflected sunlight.

The Sun is 400 times larger than the Moon but is 400 times further away from Earth making them appear the same size.

A day in Mercury lasts approximately as long as 59 days on earth.

The stars in each constellation are named after a Greek alphabet.

The first rockets were made 1,000 years ago in China.

Visit

BABY PROFESSOR
EDUCATION KIDS

www.BabyProfessorBooks.com
to download Free Baby Professor eBooks
and view our catalog of new and exciting
Children's Books